Knowing God Through the Psalms

A 6-Lesson Study
with Daily Questions

by

Kathy Rowland

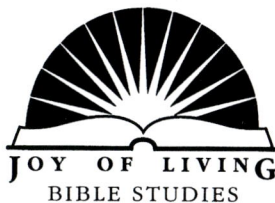

JOY OF LIVING
BIBLE STUDIES

Published by **Joy of Living Bible Studies**

For a free catalog please contact us at:

800-999-2703 or 805-650-0838

info@joyofliving.org • www.joyofliving.org

ISBN   978-1-948126-38-0

About Joy of Living

For over 45 years Joy of Living has been effectively establishing individuals around the world in the sound, basic study of God's Word.

Evangelical and interdenominational, Joy of Living reaches across denominational and cultural barriers, enriching lives through the simple, pure truths of God's inspired Word, the Bible.

Our goal is...

To help people enter into a joyous, intimate relationship with God the Father, as they come to know His Son, Jesus Christ, as Lord and Savior.

To help believers discover the fulfillment and joy that comes from daily Bible study and personal devotional time with the Lord.

To enrich lives by helping people know, understand, and apply to their lives the truths in God's inspired Word, the Bible.

To help believers grow in the grace and knowledge of our Lord and Savior Jesus Christ, so that they may please Him in every way, and experience the abundant life He has promised to His people.

To build confidence and enthusiasm in believers for sharing their faith and the joy of knowing the Lord with others.

To provide Bible study materials, at a reasonable cost, to those desiring to study God's Word, and to those desiring to teach the truth of God's Word to others.

Table of Contents

☙❧

How much better to get wisdom than gold, to choose understanding rather than silver!

Proverbs 16:16

Do You KNOW You Have Eternal Life?

Your condition...

For all have sinned and fall short of the glory of God. (Romans 3:23)

But your iniquities (sins) have separated you from your God. (Isaiah 59:2)

For the wages of sin is death. (Romans 6:23)

There is help...

For Christ died for sins once for all, the righteous for the unrighteous, to bring you to God. (1 Peter 3:18)

The gift of God is eternal life in Christ Jesus our Lord. (Romans 6:23)

What do I do?...

Repent, then, and turn to God, so that your sins may be wiped out. (Acts 3:19)

Believe in the Lord Jesus, and you will be saved. (Acts 16:31)

You CAN know...

He who has the Son has life; he who does not have the Son of God does not have life. I write these things to you who believe in the name of the Son of God so that you may know that you have eternal life. (1 John 5:12-13)

If you would like to make the decision today to repent and trust Christ as your Savior, either for the first time or as a re-commitment of your life, you may want to pray a prayer similar to this one:

Lord Jesus, I admit that I am a sinner. Please forgive my sins. Thank You for dying on the cross for me, and for coming alive again. I accept Your gifts of forgiveness and eternal life. I place my life in Your hands. I want to be Yours forever. Thank you for loving me so much.

In Your Name I pray,
Amen

How to Use This Study

Only a Bible is needed for this study.

· The Bible verses referenced each day are listed for your convenience on the right hand side of the second page of each lesson day. When possible, we suggest you read the verses in their entirety in your own Bible.

· The additional reading at the bottom of that same page is not part of the daily study, but has been provided for those who want to explore the subject more thoroughly.

As you work through each lesson, it is important to allow the Holy Spirit to reveal God's truth to you and to help you apply it to your own life and circumstances. If desired, you may consult additional commentaries after answering the questions in the lesson.

We strongly suggest that you work through the weekly lesson on a consistent daily basis rather than attempting to complete an entire lesson at one time. As you work through each daily lesson, pray and ask God to help you know, understand, and apply His truth to your life.

Remember, the point of Bible study is to know God and to build your relationship with Him.

To Use in a Group Setting:

After the daily personal study questions have been completed, the students gather in a small group, where they pray together and discuss what they have written in response to the questions, clarifying problem areas and gaining more insight into what was studied. The small group/discussion leader helps the group focus on biblical truth, and not just on personal problems. The student is the only person who sees their own answers and shares only what they feel comfortable sharing.

After small groups meet for discussion and prayer, they often gather in a large group meeting where a teacher gives a brief lecture covering the essential teaching of what was studied during the prior week and discussed in the small groups. The teacher may clarify what was studied and challenge class members to live a more committed daily life.

At home, the student begins the next lesson, reading the Bible passages and answering the questions.

A Good Place to Start...

We often hear the question, "What study should I do first? Where in the Bible should I start?"

Second Timothy 3:16 states, "All Scripture is God-breathed and is useful for teaching, rebuking, correcting and training in righteousness." There is no "bad" place to begin, because the Holy Spirit can and will use any portion of Scripture[1] to accomplish His purpose (see Isaiah 55:10-11). There are, however, some truths and starting points that may make studying the Bible easier.

WHAT
Should I Study?

WHERE
Should I Begin?

Whether you are opening the Word of God for the first time, or you've been studying for many years, we hope that this study will deepen your understanding of God and His Word and lay a foundation that will enrich your continued study.

Many of the truths that are presented in this study may not be new to you. However, if you will take the time to work through the lessons, we believe you will develop a greater understanding that will enable you to confidently share your faith with others, and help you develop a pattern of daily study.

Make a daily appointment with God. Find a quiet spot. Take your Bible and this study with you. If you have a busy phone, mute it or turn it off! Remember how very important your appointment with God is, and make time to be with Him daily. Ask yourself the following things:

How much time will I spend with the Lord each day?

What do I need to put aside in order to spend this time with the Lord? (Examples: texting, TV, digital games, etc.) Each person will have to decide what his or her priorities are and what can be removed from the daily schedule to make time to spend with God.

What is the best time for my appointment with God?

Where is the quietest place for me to pray and study?

Do I really want to spend time with God? If you do, He will help you find the time.

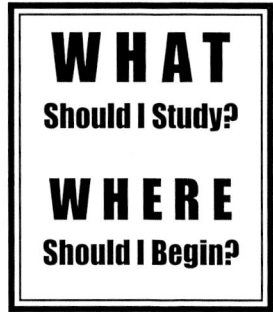

---

[1] The terms "Bible", "Word of God", and "Scripture" are used interchangeably in this study.

Lesson 1 — God Is Sovereign

"Sovereign" means having supreme power or authority.

- He is Creator.
- He is King.
- He rules now, though creation is in rebellion.
- He will judge evil.
- He will reward the godly.
- He will establish His righteous rule on earth.

Remember, as you work through each day's study, pray and ask God to help you know, understand, and apply His truth to your life.

God Is Sovereign - Day One

Read: Psalm 33:6-7 • Psalm 95:6-8a • John 7:16-17 • Psalm 119:73 •
Psalm 146:5-6

The book of Psalms is the hymnbook of Israel. The 150 collected psalms praise the Lord, His Word, and His goodness.

In this study we will look at some of the themes found in Psalms. The Lesson 1 theme is "God is Sovereign." Today we will see what the psalmists say about God the Creator.

Many psalms proclaim that God reigns or rules over everything. In other words, He is *sovereign*. This is because He is the Creator. He made everything that exists, and His power maintains all that He created.

• **From** today's Bible verses (printed on the right side of the next page), list some of the things that God created.

• **If** you have time, read the Bible passages listed under Additional reading on the next page. What else do you learn about God the Creator?[1]

• **From** Psalm 95:6-8a (at right), what are we called to do and why?

---

[1] In Psalm 74:13b-14, when referring to "the monster" and "Leviathan," the psalmist chose the language of Canaanite mythology to celebrate Yahweh's victory over the nations. (Frank E. Gaebelein, editor. *The Expositor's Bible Commentary* (Grand Rapids: Zondervan, 1990).

Creation witnesses to God's existence. His Word, the Bible, also tells us this truth. Yet many still choose to deny God's existence.

• **Do** you believe that what He says through His creation and through His Word is true? Why or why not? From John 7:16-17, what did Jesus say was the prerequisite to knowing if what He taught was from God? If you have doubts—but truly want to know if it is true in order to know and obey God—ask Him to show you His truth, and He will do it.

• **What** does Psalm 119:73 ask Him to give us?

• **From** Psalm 146:5-6, how will God care for His people, and for how long? He is able to do this because He is the Creator and He is sovereign. If you would like to, write these verses in your own words, putting your name into the passage.

• **Take** time now to thank and praise God for all of Creation. What aspects of His creation and His continuing care for it are most meaningful to you?

Today's Bible Reading

[6] By the word of the Lord the heavens were made, their starry host by the breath of his mouth. [7] He gathers the waters of the sea into jars; he puts the deep into storehouses.
— Psalm 33:6-7

[6] Come, let us bow down in worship, let us kneel before the Lord our Maker; [7] for he is our God and we are the people of his pasture, the flock under his care. Today, if only you would hear his voice, [8] "Do not harden your hearts…"
— Psalm 95:6-8a

Jesus answered, "My teaching is not my own. It comes from the one who sent me. Anyone who chooses to do the will of God will find out whether my teaching comes from God or whether I speak on my own.
— John 7:16-17

Your hands made me and formed me; give me understanding to learn your commands.
— Psalm 119:73

[5] Blessed are those whose help is the God of Jacob, whose hope is in the Lord their God. [6] He is the Maker of heaven and earth, the sea, and everything in them—he remains faithful forever.
— Psalm 146:5-6

Additional reading:
Genesis 1-2
Psalm 74:12-17
Psalm 100

God Is Sovereign - Day Two

Read: Psalm 9:7-8 • Psalm 67:4 • Psalm 74:12 • Psalm 103:2-5 • Psalm 145:13

Today we will look at how the Psalms testify that God is King over everything in heaven and on earth.

- **From** Psalm 9:8 and Psalm 67:4, over whom does God rule?

- **From** the same verses, how does the Lord rule? Look up "equity" in the dictionary.

- **As** their King, the Lord redeems His people. He acts on their behalf. What do Psalm 74:12 and Psalm 103:2-5 say about this?

- **What** is most meaningful to you today from the list in Psalm 103:2-5 of benefits God bestows on us? Why not write a prayer here, thanking Him for these things?

- **From** Psalm 9:7 and Psalm 145:13, how long will God's kingdom stand?

- **How** does it make you feel to know that God is and always will be King over everything in heaven and on earth? How will you live your life differently in light of this knowledge?

Today's Bible Reading

He rules the world in righteousness and judges the peoples with equity.

— Psalm 9:8

May the nations be glad and sing for joy, for you rule the peoples with equity and guide the nations of the earth.

— Psalm 67:4

But God is my King from long ago; he brings salvation on the earth.

— Psalm 74:12

² Praise the Lord, my soul, and forget not all his benefits—

³ who forgives all your sins and heals all your diseases,

⁴ who redeems your life from the pit and crowns you with love and compassion,

⁵ who satisfies your desires with good things so that your youth is renewed like the eagle's.

— Psalm 103:2-5

The Lord reigns forever; he has established his throne for judgment.

— Psalm 9:7

Your kingdom is an everlasting kingdom, and your dominion endures through all generations.

— Psalm 145:13

God Is Sovereign - Day Three

Read: Psalm 106:7-8,13-15 • Psalm107:10-15

Even though creation is in rebellion against God, He rules today. Because of sin, the natural inclination of all people is to turn aside from God's truth and go their own way (see Romans 3:10-12). The psalmists illustrated this pattern by looking back at the behavior of their own people, Israel.

• **From** Psalm 106:7-8, how did the Israelites rebel against God? Why did He save them from the Egyptians?

• **In** Psalm 106:13-15, what was their next step of rebellion? How did God respond this time?

God saved His people from Egyptian slavery in spite of their rebellion. But later in the wilderness, He gave them what they asked for—and their craving ended in sickness. Today we also easily forget God's many kindnesses to us. At times He sends trouble into our pathway, just to get our attention.

• **How** has God been kind to you? Do you sometimes forget to listen to Him? How has He called you back into fellowship with Him?

• **From** Psalm 107:10-15, where did some people find themselves, and why were they there?

- **What** did they finally do, and what happened then?

- **What** was their response to the Lord for His powerful intervention?

Stop and think about how God loves you. He doesn't care whether you are a failure or a success by human standards. He has already provided everything you need in Jesus Christ. (See page 4 if you aren't sure what this means.)

The first thing to do is to give thanks for that fact. Then allow His love to free you from your fears and distress.

- **Write** a prayer to the Lord here. Tell Him what you have learned about Him and about yourself today. Ask Him to help you to trust Him and to stay in relationship with Him no matter what your circumstances.

Today's Bible Reading

[7] When our ancestors were in Egypt, they gave no thought to your miracles; they did not remember your many kindnesses, and they rebelled by the sea, the Red Sea. [8] Yet he saved them for his name's sake, to make his mighty power known…

[13] But they soon forgot what he had done and did not wait for his plan to unfold. [14] In the desert they gave in to their craving; in the wilderness they put God to the test. [15] So he gave them what they asked for, but sent a wasting disease among them.

— Psalm 106:7-8,13-15

[10] Some sat in darkness, in utter darkness, prisoners suffering in iron chains, [11] because they rebelled against God's commands and despised the plans of the Most High. [12] So he subjected them to bitter labor; they stumbled, and there was no one to help.

[13] Then they cried to the Lord in their trouble, and he saved them from their distress. [14] He brought them out of darkness, the utter darkness, and broke away their chains.

[15] Let them give thanks to the Lord for his unfailing love and his wonderful deeds for mankind.

— Psalm 107:10-15

Additional reading:
Psalm 76
Romans 3:10-12

God Is Sovereign - Day Four

Read: Psalm 9:7-8 • Psalm 9:16-20 • Psalm 51:3-4

Today we will look at what the Psalms tell us about how God judges evil.

• **From** Psalm 9:7-8, since God is King, what does He have the right to do regarding all people?

From Psalm 9:16-20:

• **How** does God act on behalf of the needy and afflicted—those whom "the nations that forget God" have oppressed?

• **When** the nations (the wicked) stand in God's presence, what will they realize and how will this affect them?

- **Read** Psalm 51:3-4. What did David, the psalmist, recognize about himself, even though he was one of God's people and loved the Lord?

Every person will be held accountable to God the King. Revelation 20:11-15 describes the final judgment of all people. Verse 15 says, "Anyone whose name was not found written in the book of life was thrown into the lake of fire." When you trust Jesus Christ as your Savior, your name is recorded in that book. (See page 4 for more information.)

- **What** do you feel when you look ahead to the final judgment? Write down your thoughts and pray about this now.

Today's Bible Reading

[7] *The Lord reigns forever; he has established his throne for judgment.*

[8] *He rules the world in righteousness and judges the peoples with equity.*

— Psalm 9:7-8

[16] *The Lord is known by his acts of justice; the wicked are ensnared by the work of their hands.*

[17] *The wicked go down to the realm of the dead, all the nations that forget God.*

[18] *But God will never forget the needy; the hope of the afflicted will never perish.*

[19] *Arise, Lord, do not let mortals triumph; let the nations be judged in your presence.*

[20] *Strike them with terror, Lord; let the nations know they are only mortal.*

— Psalm 9:16-20

[3] *For I know my transgressions, and my sin is always before me.*

[4] *Against you, you only, have I sinned and done what is evil in your sight; so you are right in your verdict and justified when you judge.*

— Psalm 51:3-4

Additional reading:
Revelation 20:11-15

God Is Sovereign - Day Five

Read: Psalm 1:1-3,6a • Psalm 5:11-12 • Psalm 32:1-2,6-7

Today we will see what the Psalms tell us about how God will reward the godly or the righteous.

- **Read** Psalm 1:1-3,6a. How does the psalmist describe the godly or righteous person in these verses?

- **Have** you experienced the joy of delighting in God and His Word? How are you "like a tree planted by streams of water"?

- **In** Psalm 32:1-2 we find another description of the righteous person. Is a person righteous or godly because they work so hard to be good? How does the psalmist say they are counted as righteous?[1]

- **Do** you know whether you are counted as righteous in God's eyes? Why or why not? (Again, see page 4 for help with this.)

---

[1] See also Romans 4:4-5, "Now to the one who works, wages are not credited as a gift but as an obligation. However, to the one who does not work but trusts God who justifies the ungodly, their faith is credited as righteousness."

- **How** do Psalm 5:11-12 and Psalm 32:6-7 describe the way God rewards the righteous person?

God does not promise that the godly person will never face suffering or adversity. But He does provide a "hiding place" for those who love Him and who turn to Him when "mighty waters" threaten them.

- **Have** you discovered this truth in your own experience? How did God protect you and enable you to stand even in the mighty waters?

- **Are** you facing suffering or adversity right now? Write a prayer here, asking God for His protection and thanking Him for it.

Today's Bible Reading

[1] Blessed is the one who does not walk in step with the wicked or stand in the way that sinners take or sit in the company of mockers, [2] but whose delight is in the law of the Lord, and who meditates on his law day and night. [3] That person is like a tree planted by streams of water, which yields its fruit in season and whose leaf does not wither—whatever they do prospers... [6] For the Lord watches over the way of the righteous...
— Psalm 1:1-3,6a

[1] Blessed is the one whose transgressions are forgiven, whose sins are covered. [2] Blessed is the one whose sin the Lord does not count against them and in whose spirit is no deceit...
— Psalm 32:1-2

[11] But let all who take refuge in you be glad; let them ever sing for joy. Spread your protection over them, that those who love your name may rejoice in you. [12] Surely, Lord, you bless the righteous; you surround them with your favor as with a shield.
— Psalm 5:11-12

[6] Therefore let all the faithful pray to you while you may be found; surely the rising of the mighty waters will not reach them. [7] You are my hiding place; you will protect me from trouble and surround me with songs of deliverance.
— Psalm 32:6-7

God Is Sovereign - Day Six

Read: Psalm 89:1-4 • Psalm 96:11-13 • Psalm 102:15-16

Because God is sovereign, He will establish His righteous rule on earth. Today we will look at what the Psalms tell us about this.

• **What** does Psalm 89:1-4 declare about God's character?

• **What** promise did God make, and how long would it last?

The writers of the New Testament demonstrated that Jesus Christ is the Messiah, the long-expected Son of David who came to earth to fulfill God's plan for the redemption of His people, and who will one day return again to earth to establish God's reign.

• **From** Psalm 96:11-13, what is all of creation looking forward to?

• **When** this event takes place, what will the Lord do?

• **In** Psalm 102:15-16, what does the psalmist say the Lord will do?

The psalmists looked forward to the establishment of Zion, built by the Lord and prepared for His servants. It will be the fulfillment of God's Kingdom on earth.

This hope is expressed so beautifully in the hymn "Jesus Shall Reign" by Isaac Watts:

Jesus shall reign wher-e'er the sun
Does his successive journeys run;
His kingdom stretch from shore to shore,
Till moons shall wax and wane no more.

• **Are** you looking forward to Zion, to the righteous reign on earth of Jesus Christ, Son of David, Messiah and Lord? Write a prayer or a poem here, expressing your thoughts.

Today's Bible Reading

¹ I will sing of the Lord's great love forever; with my mouth I will make your faithfulness known through all generations.

² I will declare that your love stands firm forever, that you have established your faithfulness in heaven itself.

³ You said, "I have made a covenant with my chosen one, I have sworn to David my servant,

⁴ 'I will establish your line forever and make your throne firm through all generations.'"

— Psalm 89:1-4

¹¹ Let the heavens rejoice, let the earth be glad; let the sea resound, and all that is in it.

¹² Let the fields be jubilant, and everything in them; let all the trees of the forest sing for joy.

¹³ Let all creation rejoice before the Lord, for he comes, he comes to judge the earth. He will judge the world in righteousness and the peoples in his faithfulness.

— Psalm 96:11-13

¹⁵ The nations will fear the name of the Lord, all the kings of the earth will revere your glory.

¹⁶ For the Lord will rebuild Zion and appear in his glory.

— Psalm 102:15-16

God Is Sovereign - Day Seven

Take a few minutes today to review the Bible verses from this week. Write down what has been most meaningful to you.

As you have worked through the study this week, we hope that you have discovered what God's sovereignty means and how important it is.

Lesson 2 — God Is Trustworthy

- He is our Father.
- He is present with us.
- He is in control.
- He will protect us.
- He is loyal and unchanging.
- He is forgiving and merciful.

꧁꧂

Remember, as you work through each day's study, pray and ask God to help you know, understand, and apply His truth to your life.

God Is Trustworthy - Day One

Read: Psalm 3 • John 10:27-29

We can trust God because He is our Father. In Psalm 3, the psalmist, King David, addresses God as "Lord," which is the translation of *Yahweh*, His revealed covenant name to the people of Israel. When Old Testament believers used this name of God, it was similar to Jesus and New Testament believers addressing God as "Abba, Father" (see Mark 14:35-36; Romans 8:15-16).

• **What** did David's foes say about his trust in the Lord in Psalm 3:1-2?

• **From** verses 3-4, even though David knew he had many foes, why did he know he could trust in the Lord?

Even though everything seems at its worst, when there is no earthly help in sight, we can take comfort that when we call out to our Father God, He *will* answer us.

• **What** was David able to do in verses 5-6? Why?

• **When** you face a multitude of problems in your own life, are you able to do this? Why or why not?

- **In** verse 4 David said that he called out to the Lord. From verse 7, what are the actual words of his prayer to *Yahweh*?[1] How does this respond to what David's enemies said in verse 2?

- **What** is the result of the Lord's deliverance of His people, according to verse 8?

David hoped for God's personal blessing for himself as Israel's king, but that was not the end of his petition. David looked forward to the time of God's full blessing coming to His people. We look forward to this too, as we trust in Jesus' promises.

- **Read** John 10:27-29. What did Jesus promise to those who believe in Him? How does this confirm David's trust in *Yahweh's* power and faithfulness to His people?

- **What** does this mean to you? Have you put your trust in your Father God to deliver you from whatever enemies and problems surround you? Why not pray about this now?

---

[1] "This expression of vindication may seem harsh to our ears, but the psalmist is putting before us the hope that, regardless what enemies may arise from within or from without the kingdom of God, God will be victorious." (*The Expositor's Bible Commentary*)

Today's Bible Reading

[1] *Lord, how many are my foes! How many rise up against me!*

[2] *Many are saying of me, "God will not deliver him."*

[3] *But you, Lord, are a shield around me, my glory, the One who lifts my head high.*

[4] *I call out to the Lord, and he answers me from his holy mountain.*

[5] *I lie down and sleep; I wake again, because the Lord sustains me.*

[6] *I will not fear though tens of thousands assail me on every side.*

[7] *Arise, Lord! Deliver me, my God! Strike all my enemies on the jaw; break the teeth of the wicked.*

[8] *From the Lord comes deliverance. May your blessing be on your people.*

— Psalm 3

[27] *My sheep listen to my voice; I know them, and they follow me.*

[28] *I give them eternal life, and they shall never perish; no one will snatch them out of my hand.*

[29] *My Father, who has given them to me, is greater than all; no one can snatch them out of my Father's hand.*

— John 10:27-29

Additional reading:
Mark 14:35-36
Romans 8:15-16

God Is Trustworthy - Day Two

Read: Psalm 27:1-5 • Matthew 6:33-34

We can trust God because He is present with us. King David expresses his confidence in the Lord's presence in Psalm 27.

• **In** Psalm 27:1, what are the ways David describes the Lord's presence with him?

• **A** stronghold is a place of refuge, like a castle or a fort. In Psalm 27:2-3, how does David express his confidence in the Lord's protecting presence?

• **What** does David long for in Psalm 27:4?

The house of the Lord was the temple in Jerusalem. It was the visible expression of God's presence with His people. But David's longing wasn't for the building, but rather for being with God Himself.

• **How** does Psalm 27:5 say this close relationship to God would affect David's life during difficult times?

David put his complete trust in God, not as a far-away heavenly policeman who would come and rescue him when called, but rather as David's dearly-loved Father God, with whom he had daily fellowship.

*   **In** Matthew 6:33-34, what did Jesus tell us should be our top priority?

*   **If** we do this, what does Jesus assure us will happen?

We are privileged to seek God's presence through reading His Word, the Bible, through speaking to Him in prayer, and through the teaching and fellowship we experience meeting with other believers.

*   **Do** you yearn for a close relationship with God? Are you seeking Him through the ways listed above? If you're not sure how this is possible, see page 4.

Today's Bible Reading

¹ The Lord is my light and my salvation—whom shall I fear? The Lord is the stronghold of my life—of whom shall I be afraid?

² When the wicked advance against me to devour me, it is my enemies and my foes who will stumble and fall.

³ Though an army besiege me, my heart will not fear; though war break out against me, even then I will be confident.

⁴ One thing I ask from the Lord, this only do I seek: that I may dwell in the house of the Lord all the days of my life, to gaze on the beauty of the Lord and to seek him in his temple.

⁵ For in the day of trouble he will keep me safe in his dwelling; he will hide me in the shelter of his sacred tent and set me high upon a rock.

— Psalm 27:1-5

³³ But seek first the kingdom of God and His righteousness, and all these things will be provided for you.

³⁴ Therefore don't worry about tomorrow, because tomorrow will worry about itself. Each day has enough trouble of its own.

— Matthew 6:33-34

God Is Trustworthy - Day Three

Read: Psalm 31:14-15 • Isaiah 33:6 • Matthew 10:29-31 • Psalm 31:23-24

We can trust God because He is in control. (Read all of Psalm 31 in your Bible if you would like to. The verses we are addressing today are printed on page 27.)

- **Read** Psalm 31:14-15. In verse 15, what phrase does David use to express the complete sovereignty of God over his life—the reason He can be trusted?

Other Scripture passages confirm this description of God.

- **How** did the prophet Isaiah describe the Lord in Isaiah 33:6?

- **In** the same verse, what did Isaiah say is the key to experiencing this truth in your own life?

- **Read** Matthew 10:29-31. How did Jesus reassure His followers that they can trust God to care for them?

Returning to Psalm 31, read verses 23-24.

- **What** does David exhort the Lord's people to do, and why?

David contrasts two kinds of people: those who are faithful to the Lord and hope in Him; and those who are proud, who trust in themselves and their circumstances, their possessions, their power, etc.

- **Be** honest with yourself. Which group of people are you a part of? Why?

- **Perhaps** you admitted that you have been trusting in yourself instead of in the Lord. Would you like to change this? Why not pray about it now?

Today's Bible Reading

14 But I trust in you, Lord; I say, "You are my God."

15 My times are in your hands; deliver me from the hands of my enemies, from those who pursue me.

— Psalm 31:14-15

He will be the sure foundation for your times, a rich store of salvation and wisdom and knowledge; the fear of the Lord is the key to this treasure.

— Isaiah 33:6

Are not two sparrows sold for a penny? Yet not one of them will fall to the ground outside your Father's care. And even the very hairs of your head are all numbered. So don't be afraid; you are worth more than many sparrows.

—Matthew 10:29-31

23 Love the Lord, all his faithful people! The Lord preserves those who are true to him, but the proud he pays back in full.

24 Be strong and take heart, all you who hope in the Lord.

— Psalm 31:23-24

God Is Trustworthy - Day Four

Read: Psalm 46 • Isaiah 26:3

We can trust God because He will protect us. Psalm 46 may sound familiar to you, since it is paraphrased in Martin Luther's great hymn, "A Mighty Fortress Is Our God."

• **In** Psalm 46:1, 7 and 11, what words does the psalmist use to picture God's presence in protecting His people?

As God's people, we always need Him, but we particularly experience His presence when we are going through difficulties.

• **What** disasters does the psalmist speak of in verses 2-3? Can you imagine yourself in the midst of such events? Would you be able to say, "Therefore I will not fear" in such terrible circumstances?

• **How** do verses 4-5 describe the city of God? This city is a picture of the people of God. Why is she safe?

• **Isaiah** 26 also describes the city of God. How does Isaiah 26:3 describe the mental and emotional state of those who trust in the Lord?

- **From** Psalm 46:6 and 8, what has God done throughout history to protect and save His people?

- **From** verse 9, what can God's people look forward to?

- **Until** the time comes when God brings about these things, what does He say in Psalm 46:10 that His people should focus on?

- **What** difficulties are you facing today? Are you able to focus on God's presence with you in the midst of them? Why not pray about this now?

[1] God is our refuge and strength, an ever-present help in trouble.

[2] Therefore we will not fear, though the earth give way and the mountains fall into the heart of the sea,

[3] though its waters roar and foam and the mountains quake with their surging.

[4] There is a river whose streams make glad the city of God, the holy place where the Most High dwells.

[5] God is within her, she will not fall; God will help her at break of day.

[6] Nations are in uproar, kingdoms fall; he lifts his voice, the earth melts.

[7] The Lord Almighty is with us; the God of Jacob is our fortress.

[8] Come and see what the Lord has done, the desolations he has brought on the earth.

[9] He makes wars cease to the ends of the earth. He breaks the bow and shatters the spear; he burns the shields with fire.

[10] He says, "Be still, and know that I am God; I will be exalted among the nations, I will be exalted in the earth."

[11] The Lord Almighty is with us; the God of Jacob is our fortress.

— Psalm 46

You will keep in perfect peace those whose minds are steadfast, because they trust in you.

—Isaiah 26:3

God Is Trustworthy - Day Five

Read: Psalm 62

We can trust God because He is loyal and unchanging. People often show themselves to be untrustworthy, but the Lord is not like that.

• **How** does David describe God in Psalm 62:1-2?

God is faithful to His people and is able to protect them through His mighty power. However, resting in Him requires waiting and patience.

• **In** Psalm 62:3-4, how do ungodly people attack David?

Verses 5-7 repeat the reasons David is confident in the Lord, the reasons he first wrote in verses 1-2.

• **In** Psalm 62:5, what does David gain from depending on God— something he didn't mention in verses 1-2?

• **What** does David call upon all of God's people to do in Psalm 62:8?

- **Psalm** 62:9-10 lists things that some people in David's time put their trust in. What are they? What do you see people trusting in today?

- **Finally,** in verses 11-12, David returns to the promises of God to His people. What are they?

Jesus said something similar in Matthew 16:27, "For the Son of Man is going to come in his Father's glory with his angels, and then he will reward each person according to what they have done."

Remember, this doesn't mean that you have to do good works to earn salvation. The only thing God wants you to do is to put your trust in Him, to trust that what He did for you in Christ Jesus is sufficient for you. (See page 4 for more information.)

- **Have** you trusted that God loves you with "unfailing" love? Have you thanked Him for what He has done for you? Write a prayer here if you would like to.

Today's Bible Reading

[1] Truly my soul finds rest in God; my salvation comes from him.

[2] Truly he is my rock and my salvation; he is my fortress, I will never be shaken.

[3] How long will you assault me? Would all of you throw me down—this leaning wall, this tottering fence?

[4] Surely they intend to topple me from my lofty place; they take delight in lies. With their mouths they bless, but in their hearts they curse.

[5] Yes, my soul, find rest in God; my hope comes from him.

[6] Truly he is my rock and my salvation; he is my fortress, I will not be shaken.

[7] My salvation and my honor depend on God; he is my mighty rock, my refuge.

[8] Trust in him at all times, you people; pour out your hearts to him, for God is our refuge.

[9] Surely the lowborn are but a breath, the highborn are but a lie. If weighed on a balance, they are nothing; together they are only a breath.

[10] Do not trust in extortion or put vain hope in stolen goods; though your riches increase, do not set your heart on them.

[11] One thing God has spoken, two things I have heard: "Power belongs to you, God,

[12] and with you, Lord, is unfailing love"; and, "You reward everyone according to what they have done."

— Psalm 62

God Is Trustworthy - Day Six

Read: Psalm 86:1-7 • Psalm 86:11-13

We can trust God because He is forgiving and merciful. In Psalm 86, David asks for God's mercy and expresses his confidence in Him. (Read the whole psalm in your Bible if you would like to. The verses we are addressing today are on printed on page 33.)

• **In** verse 1, how does David describe himself? Remember, David was king of Israel when he wrote this. Does this self-description fit your idea of a king's situation? Consider that he may be describing his spiritual condition.

• **From** verses 2-3, how does David describe his relationship to God?

• **What** does David receive from God when he calls to Him, according to verses 4 and 5?

• **From** verses 6-7, what is David certain that God will do in response to his prayer?

When we trust in the Lord, we are able to look beyond whatever our current troubles are. We focus on God, the source of our peace and security.

- **How** does David express this confidence in the Lord in Psalm 86:11-13?

Jesus, the Son of God, confirmed that we can trust in Him no matter what troubles we face. He said in John 16:33, "I have told you these things, so that in me you may have peace. In this world you will have trouble. But take heart! I have overcome the world."

- **Do** you rest in God's peace because of Who He is? Do you trust that because Jesus has "overcome the world," the world cannot overcome you? Write down your thoughts about this.

Today's Bible Reading

1 Hear me, Lord, and answer me, for I am poor and needy.

2 Guard my life, for I am faithful to you; save your servant who trusts in you. You are my God;

3 have mercy on me, Lord, for I call to you all day long.

4 Bring joy to your servant, Lord, for I put my trust in you.

5 You, Lord, are forgiving and good, abounding in love to all who call to you.

6 Hear my prayer, Lord; listen to my cry for mercy.

7 When I am in distress, I call to you, because you answer me.

— Psalm 86:1-7

11 Teach me your way, Lord, that I may rely on your faithfulness; give me an undivided heart, that I may fear your name.

12 I will praise you, Lord my God, with all my heart; I will glorify your name forever.

13 For great is your love toward me; you have delivered me from the depths, from the realm of the dead.

— Psalm 86:11-13

God Is Trustworthy - Day Seven

Take a few minutes today to review the Bible verses from this week. Write down what has been most meaningful to you.

As you have worked through the study this week, we hope that you have a deeper understanding of God's trustworthiness and what it means to you.

Lesson 3 — God Is Praiseworthy

- His majesty is revealed in Creation.
- Creation praises its Maker.
- He is the victorious King.
- Praise Him continually out of a grateful heart.
- He reigns from all eternity.
- His covenant is with His people.

⁕

Remember, as you work through each day's study, pray and ask God to help you know, understand, and apply His truth to your life.

God Is Praiseworthy - Day One

Read: Psalm 8

The theme of many of the Psalms is purely praise to God. In Psalm 8, David's praise focuses on God's majesty revealed in creation.

- **From** Psalm 8:1, where in creation is the Lord's majesty revealed? Compare this to Paul's words in Romans 1:20 (see page 39).

- **Although** there are enemies in the midst of God's creation, whose praise will silence them, according to Psalm 8:2? Jesus quoted this verse in Matthew 21:15-16.

- **In** Psalm 8:3-4, how does David contrast the two spheres of God's rule— heaven and earth? If you would like to, read Genesis 1:27-28. What did God set mankind to rule over?

- **David** continues in Psalm 8:5-9 to describe humanity's significance given to us by God. What did God do?

In Hebrews 2:6-9, the writer quotes from Psalm 8 and points out that Jesus is the fulfillment of God's intention for humanity. Jesus, the Son of Man, suffered death on our behalf, and is now crowned with the full glory and honor God has reserved for humanity.

- **Do** you ever "consider the heavens"? What do you see there that testifies to God's majesty?

- **What** responsibility do you think God has given you, as one of the "rulers over the works of [God's] hands"?

- **If** you would like to, write your own prayer or psalm of praise to God regarding His majesty revealed in Creation.

Today's Bible Reading

¹ *Lord, our Lord, how majestic is your name in all the earth! You have set your glory in the heavens.*

² *Through the praise of children and infants you have established a stronghold against your enemies, to silence the foe and the avenger.*

³ *When I consider your heavens, the work of your fingers, the moon and the stars, which you have set in place,*

⁴ *what is mankind that you are mindful of them, human beings that you care for them?*

⁵ *You have made them a little lower than the angels and crowned them with glory and honor.*

⁶ *You made them rulers over the works of your hands; you put everything under their feet:*

⁷ *all flocks and herds, and the animals of the wild,*

⁸ *the birds in the sky, and the fish in the sea, all that swim the paths of the seas.*

⁹ *Lord, our Lord, how majestic is your name in all the earth!*
— Psalm 8

Additional reading:
Matthew 21:15-16
Genesis 1:27-28
Hebrews 2:6-9

God Is Praiseworthy - Day Two

Read: Psalm 19:1-6 • Romans 1:18-20

The first part of Psalm 19 focuses on the Creation praising its Maker. (We will study the second part of the psalm in Lesson 4.)

• **In** Psalm 19:1-4a, what do the heavens say about God? How do they reveal this?

• **From** the same verses, can anyone, anywhere, truthfully say they have never learned anything of God?

• **In** Romans 1:18-20, how does Paul explicitly confirm this?

Paul's purpose in this passage was not to write off as lost the people who have not recognized God's majesty through the creation. Rather, he goes on in his letter to the Romans to proclaim the deliverance and salvation God has made available through Jesus Christ. (For example, read Romans 3:22-26.)

- **What** does Psalm 19:4b-6 say about the sun?

- **How** does this regularity support life on earth? What do you think this reveals about God?

C.S. Lewis wrote, "I take [Psalm 19] to be the greatest poem in the Psalter and one of the greatest lyrics in the world."[1]

- **Read** Psalm 19:1-6 again as a poem. How did the psalmist's writing delight or impress you? Can you see why this and other psalms have inspired so many creative works of art and music?

Today's Bible Reading

[1] The heavens declare the glory of God; the skies proclaim the work of his hands.

[2] Day after day they pour forth speech; night after night they reveal knowledge.

[3] They have no speech, they use no words; no sound is heard from them.

[4] Yet their voice goes out into all the earth, their words to the ends of the world. In the heavens God has pitched a tent for the sun.

[5] It is like a bridegroom coming out of his chamber, like a champion rejoicing to run his course.

[6] It rises at one end of the heavens and makes its circuit to the other; nothing is deprived of its warmth.

— Psalm 19:1-6

[18] The wrath of God is being revealed from heaven against all the godlessness and wickedness of people, who suppress the truth by their wickedness, [19] since what may be known about God is plain to them, because God has made it plain to them. [20] For since the creation of the world God's invisible qualities—his eternal power and divine nature—have been clearly seen, being understood from what has been made, so that people are without excuse.

— Romans 1:18-20

Additional reading:
Romans 3:22-26

---

1. Lewis, C.S. *Reflections on the Psalms*. London: Geoffrey Bles, 1958, p. 63.

God Is Praiseworthy - Day Three

Read: Psalm 29

David praises the Lord as the victorious King in Psalm 29.

- **In** verses 1-2, what does the psalmist call on the "heavenly beings," or angels, to do?

- **What** earthly illustrations does David use to illustrate the majesty and power of God in verses 3-9a?[1]

God's "voice" is mentioned seven times in verses 3-9. In addition to His mighty works in nature and in Israel's history, God revealed Himself to His people by audibly speaking to them at Mount Sinai. If you would like, you can read about it in Exodus 19:10-19.

- **From** Psalm 29:9b, how do the heavenly beings in God's temple respond to His splendor?

---

1. In verses 5-6, "Lebanon" and "Sirion" (Hermon) are the mountain ranges north of Israel.

- **Although** God's glory is displayed in nature as awesome power, what assurance does David give God's people in Psalm 29:10-11?

Jesus, God's only Son, gave the same assurance to His followers in John 14:27, "Peace I leave with you; my peace I give you. I do not give to you as the world gives. Do not let your hearts be troubled and do not be afraid."

- **Have** you joined the angels in praising God for His glorious power and majesty? Write your praise here, if you'd like to.

- **How** have you experienced the strength and peace that God gives to His people even during tumultuous times? Share with your discussion group if you would like to.

Today's Bible Reading

[1] Ascribc to thc Lord, you heavenly beings, ascribe to the Lord glory and strength.

[2] Ascribe to the Lord the glory due his name; worship the Lord in the splendor of his holiness.

[3] The voice of the Lord is over the waters; the God of glory thunders, the Lord thunders over the mighty waters.

[4] The voice of the Lord is powerful; the voice of the Lord is majestic.

[5] The voice of the Lord breaks the cedars; the Lord breaks in pieces the cedars of Lebanon.

[6] He makes Lebanon leap like a calf, Sirion like a young wild ox.

[7] The voice of the Lord strikes with flashes of lightning.

[8] The voice of the Lord shakes the desert; the Lord shakes the Desert of Kadesh.

[9] The voice of the Lord twists the oaks and strips the forests bare. And in his temple all cry, "Glory!"

[10] The Lord sits enthroned over the flood; the Lord is enthroned as King forever.

[11] The Lord gives strength to his people; the Lord blesses his people with peace.

— Psalm 29

Additional reading:
Exodus 19:10-19

God Is Praiseworthy - Day Four

Read: Psalm 34:1-10 • Hebrews 13:15

In Psalm 34, the psalmist calls all God's people to praise Him continually out of a grateful heart.

• **What** is David's personal focus in verses 1-2?

• **What** does he call God's people to do in verse 3?

• **From** Hebrews 13:15, what is the sacrifice Christians offer to the Lord, and how often do we offer it?

• **In** Psalm 34:4 and 6, what did David do when he was afraid, and how did God respond?

- **When** God's people turn to the Lord, what is the result, from verses 5 and 7?

- **In** Psalm 34:8-10, what must God's people do in order to experience His goodness?

- **Do** you find yourself praising the Lord continually out of a grateful heart? Do you long to meet with God's people and praise Him together? If not, why not?

- **How** have you experienced the Lord saving you from your fears and troubles? Share with your group if you would like to.

Today's Bible Reading

¹ *I will extol the Lord at all times; his praise will always be on my lips.*

² *I will glory in the Lord; let the afflicted hear and rejoice.*

³ *Glorify the Lord with me; let us exalt his name together.*

⁴ *I sought the Lord, and he answered me; he delivered me from all my fears.*

⁵ *Those who look to him are radiant; their faces are never covered with shame.*

⁶ *This poor man called, and the Lord heard him; he saved him out of all his troubles.*

⁷ *The angel of the Lord encamps around those who fear him, and he delivers them.*

⁸ *Taste and see that the Lord is good; blessed is the one who takes refuge in him.*

⁹ *Fear the Lord, you his holy people, for those who fear him lack nothing.*

¹⁰ *The lions may grow weak and hungry, but those who seek the Lord lack no good thing.*

— Psalm 34:1-10

Through Jesus, therefore, let us continually offer to God a sacrifice of praise—the fruit of lips that openly profess his name.

— Hebrews 13:15

God Is Praiseworthy - Day Five

Read: Psalm 93 • Revelation 19:6 • Exodus 29:45-46 • Matthew 1:23

Psalm 93 praises the Lord for His reign over the world from all eternity.

• **How** does the psalmist describe God's reign in Psalm 93:1?

• **Compare** this to the Apostle John's description in Revelation 19:6 of what will take place in heaven at the end of time.

• **In** Psalm 93:2, the psalmist declares that God's throne over the earth was established "long ago"—at the time He created it. But in contrast, what does he say is the length of God's own existence?

• **How** is God's kingship over the seas celebrated in Psalm 93:3-4?

- **In** Psalm 93:5, how does the psalmist describe the rule of the Lord among His people?

- **From** Exodus 29:45-46, how was the Lord going to relate to His people?

The majestic God who created the earth would, amazingly, dwell among His people. His statutes—His covenant—stand firm forever. This was confirmed in His Son, Jesus Christ.

- **Read** Matthew 1:23. What Old Testament prophecy was fulfilled in Jesus? What would He be called, and why?

- **Are** you one of God's people? (See page 4 for more information.) Have you experienced His presence dwelling within you through His Holy Spirit? Why not pray now and praise Him?

Today's Bible Reading

[1] *The Lord reigns, he is robed in majesty; the Lord is robed in majesty and armed with strength; indeed, the world is established, firm and secure.*

[2] *Your throne was established long ago; you are from all eternity.*

[3] *The seas have lifted up, Lord, the seas have lifted up their voice; the seas have lifted up their pounding waves.*

[4] *Mightier than the thunder of the great waters, mightier than the breakers of the sea—the Lord on high is mighty.*

[5] *Your statutes, Lord, stand firm; holiness adorns your house for endless days.*

— Psalm 93

Then I heard what sounded like a great multitude, like the roar of rushing waters and like loud peals of thunder, shouting: "Hallelujah! For our Lord God Almighty reigns."

— Revelation 19:6

[45] *Then I will dwell among the Israelites and be their God.*

[45] *They will know that I am the Lord their God, who brought them out of Egypt so that I might dwell among them. I am the Lord their God.*

— Exodus 29:45-46

The virgin will conceive and give birth to a son, and they will call him Immanuel" *(which means "God with us").*

—Matthew 1:23

God Is Praiseworthy - Day Six

Read: Psalm 100 • Isaiah 56:6-7 • 1 John 4:10

One of the most familiar psalms, Psalm 100 praises God for His covenant relationship with His people.

• **Who** is called to praise the Lord in Psalm 100:1-2, and how are they to do it?

Sometimes we think that in the Old Testament, only the people of Israel were invited to be in relationship with God.

• **Read** Isaiah 56:6-7. How are non-Israelites invited to follow the Lord?

• **From** Psalm 100:3, what do the Lord's people know about Him? What word-picture does the psalmist use to describe God's relationship to His people?

• **Jesus** described how much the good shepherd values each sheep in Luke 15:3-6. If you would like to, look up these verses and summarize them.

Just as in Psalm 100:1-2, verse 4 again urges God's people to thank and praise Him.

- **What** does the psalmist say in verse 5 are amazing reasons to praise the Lord?

So many of the reasons God is praiseworthy have focused on His creativity, majesty, and power, and rightfully so. But here the psalmist celebrates God's love and faithfulness.

- **Read** 1 John 4:10. How did God show His love and faithfulness to His people in the most amazing way?

- **Have** you accepted God's gift of His Son as the sacrifice that paid for all your sin? Do you daily thank and praise Him for this? Whom do you need to share this good news with?

Today's Bible Reading

¹ Shout for joy to the Lord, all the earth.

² Worship the Lord with gladness; come before him with joyful songs.

³ Know that the Lord is God. It is he who made us, and we are his; we are his people, the sheep of his pasture.

⁴ Enter his gates with thanksgiving and his courts with praise; give thanks to him and praise his name.

⁵ For the Lord is good and his love endures forever; his faithfulness continues through all generations.

— Psalm 100

⁶ And foreigners who bind themselves to the Lord to minister to him, to love the name of the Lord, and to be his servants, all who keep the Sabbath without desecrating it and who hold fast to my covenant—

⁷ these I will bring to my holy mountain and give them joy in my house of prayer. Their burnt offerings and sacrifices will be accepted on my altar; for my house will be called a house of prayer for all nations. "

— Isaiah 56:6-7

This is love: not that we loved God, but that he loved us and sent his Son as an atoning sacrifice for our sins.

—1 John 4:10

Additional reading:
Luke 15:3-6

God Is Praiseworthy - Day Seven

Take a few minutes today to review the Bible verses from this week. Write down what has been most meaningful to you.

We hope that you are knowing and understanding more about God, and that you are learning how to praise Him in everything.

Lesson 4 — God's Law Is a Delight

- Meditating on it brings blessing.
- All of God's law is beneficial.
- Seek Him with a whole heart.
- Living by God's law keeps us pure.
- His unfailing love is promised.
- Long to lead others to love it.

৵৽৶

*Remember, as you work through each day's study,
pray and ask God to help you know, understand,
and apply His truth to your life.*

God's Law Is a Delight - Day One

Read: Psalm 1 • Matthew 6:9-10

In the Psalms, God's "law" is not limited to the Five Books of Moses, or even to the Old Testament as a whole. Rather, it is all of His instruction—His Word to His people, given to help us live in harmony with His will.[1]

• **From** Psalm 1:1, what activities and attitudes will a person avoid if they want to experience God's blessing?

• **What** does that person delight in, according to Psalm 1:2? How often do they think about it?

• **Jesus** also taught us to search for and delight in doing God's will. What do you learn about this in Matthew 6:9-10?

• **In** Psalm 1:3, how is the godly person's life portrayed? From verse 6a, why is this true?

1. *The Expositor's Bible Commentary*. See notes on Psalm 1:2.

- **What** is the picture of the ungodly person's life in Psalm 1:4? From verses 5 and 6b, what will be their final destination?

God's blessing upon His people doesn't necessarily bring worldly prosperity, but always brings joy and gratitude as we live in fellowship with Him.

- **Do** you delight in God's Word? When and how do you meditate on it?

- **How** would you describe the blessing you receive from this fellowship with the Lord?

Today's Bible Reading

[1] Blessed is the one who does not walk in step with the wicked or stand in the way that sinners take or sit in the company of mockers,

[2] but whose delight is in the law of the Lord, and who meditates on his law day and night.

[3] That person is like a tree planted by streams of water, which yields its fruit in season and whose leaf does not wither—whatever they do prospers.

[4] Not so the wicked! They are like chaff that the wind blows away.

[5] Therefore the wicked will not stand in the judgment, nor sinners in the assembly of the righteous.

[6] For the Lord watches over the way of the righteous, but the way of the wicked leads to destruction.

— Psalm 1

[9] This, then, is how you should pray: "Our Father in heaven, hallowed be your name, [10] your kingdom come, your will be done, on earth as it is in heaven."

— Matthew 6:9-10

God's Law Is a Delight - Day Two

Read: Psalm 19:7-14

In Lesson 3 we studied Psalm 19:1-6, which focused on the revelation of God through creation as it praises its Creator. Now, in verses 7-14, we will see how God's revelation through His law is beneficial to His people.

- **How** does David, the psalmist, describe God's law in verses 7-8? (Look at the first part of each sentence.)

- **What** benefits does God's law offer, from the second part of each sentence in verses 7-8?

- **From** verse 9, what do we need in order to benefit from God's law? How long will these benefits last?

- **From** verses 10-11, how valuable and desirable is God's law?

David now turns to thoughts of himself in relation to God and His revelation.

- **In** verses 12-13, what two types of sin is he concerned about? How does he ask God to help him with these?

- **Are** you concerned about these two types of sin in your own life? Write down your thoughts, and pray about this now if you would like to.

- **What** is David's prayer in verse 14?

God loves to have us meditate on His Word and speak to Him in prayer, just as David did.

- **How** precious is it to you that you are able to know God through His Word, and be in relationship with Him? Write down your thoughts.

Today's Bible Reading

[7] The law of the Lord is perfect, refreshing the soul. The statutes of the Lord are trustworthy, making wise the simple.

[8] The precepts of the Lord are right, giving joy to the heart. The commands of the Lord are radiant, giving light to the eyes.

[9] The fear of the Lord is pure, enduring forever. The decrees of the Lord are firm, and all of them are righteous.

[10] They are more precious than gold, than much pure gold; they are sweeter than honey, than honey from the honeycomb.

[11] By them your servant is warned; in keeping them there is great reward.

[12] But who can discern their own errors? Forgive my hidden faults.

[13] Keep your servant also from willful sins; may they not rule over me. Then I will be blameless, innocent of great transgression.

[14] May these words of my mouth and this meditation of my heart be pleasing in your sight, Lord, my Rock and my Redeemer.

— Psalm 19:7-14

God's Law Is a Delight - Day Three

Read: Psalm 119:1-8 • Deuteronomy 6:5 • 1 Kings 8:39b

Psalm 119, known for its teaching on God's law, contains 22 stanzas of 8 verses each. We will study 4 of the stanzas for the remainder of this lesson.

No human except Jesus Christ is or has been perfect. Faith has always been the foundation of our acceptance with God (see Ephesians 2:8). In the Old Testament Israel came to God by various sacrifices. These sacrifices did not take away their sin (see Hebrews 10:4), but as they offered them in faith, they covered their sin. All these sacrifices pointed toward the perfect sacrifice that would be revealed in the New Testament: Jesus Christ, the Lamb of God who takes away the sin of the world (see John 1:29). Today's verses do not refer to a sinless person, but to a person who has come to God by faith in Christ.

• **What** brings God's blessing to a person, according to Psalm 119:1-4?

• **You** may think, "Whose ways can ever be blameless?"[1] The key is found in verse 2b. What does God look for in a person that brings His blessing?

• **How** did Moses express this in Deuteronomy 6:5?

We obey God *because* we love Him, not in order to *earn* His blessing.

• **What** is the psalmist's prayer in Psalm 119:5-6?

---

[1] *Blameless* does not mean *sinless*. It means we keep our hearts as clean as possible by confessing our sins regularly to the Lord and repenting of them.

The psalmist prays for God's mercy, hoping that his response to God's revelation is acceptable.

- **God** judges our response to His revelation, not by whether we are able to obey it perfectly, but by whether our hearts are seeking Him. What does 1 Kings 8:39b say about this?

- **From** Psalm 119:7, what will the psalmist do as he is assured of God's favor?

- **What** does he ask the Lord in verse 8?

- **If** you have time, read Isaiah 49:14-16. What do you learn about whether God will *ever* forsake His people?

Today's Bible Reading

[1] Blessed are those whose ways are blameless, who walk according to the law of the Lord.

[2] Blessed are those who keep his statutes and seek him with all their heart—

[3] they do no wrong but follow his ways.

[4] You have laid down precepts that are to be fully obeyed.

[5] Oh, that my ways were steadfast in obeying your decrees!

[6] Then I would not be put to shame when I consider all your commands.

[7] I will praise you with an upright heart as I learn your righteous laws.

[8] I will obey your decrees; do not utterly forsake me.

— Psalm 119:1-8

Love the Lord your God with all your heart and with all your soul and with all your strength.

— Deuteronomy 6:5

...Forgive and act; deal with everyone according to all they do, since you know their hearts (for you alone know every human heart).

— 1 Kings 8:39b

Additional reading:
Isaiah 49:14-16
John 1:29
Ephesians 2:8
Hebrews 10:4

God's Law Is a Delight - Day Four

Read: Psalm 119:9-16 • Ecclesiastes 12:1

Today we'll look at the second stanza of Psalm 119.

• **What** advice does the psalmist give to a young person in verse 9?

• **Of** course, this advice pertains to a person of any age, but what do you think are the benefits of starting at a younger age? How would you express this to a child or teenager that you know?

• **How** does Ecclesiastes 12:1 confirm this advice?

• **From** Psalm 119:10, what is the psalmist's attitude towards the Lord? What help does he ask from God?

• **What** action can we take that will help us to keep from sinning? (Psalm 119:11)

- **Do** you memorize Scripture passages regularly? How have they helped you stay on God's path? Share with your group if you would like to.

- **In** Psalm 119:12-13, the psalmist asks God's help to learn and remember His decrees, and also speaks of them to others. How can you do this in your own life?

- **To** what does the psalmist compare the experience of following God's statutes, in Psalm 119:14? Could you say the same thing—for example, if you compare following God's law to winning a huge lottery prize?

- **From** Psalm 119:15-16, how is the psalmist's love for the Lord expressed through his actions and attitudes?

Today's Bible Reading

⁹ How can a young person stay on the path of purity? By living according to your word.

¹⁰ I seek you with all my heart; do not let me stray from your commands.

¹¹ I have hidden your word in my heart that I might not sin against you.

¹² Praise be to you, Lord; teach me your decrees.

¹³ With my lips I recount all the laws that come from your mouth.

¹⁴ I rejoice in following your statutes as one rejoices in great riches.

¹⁵ I meditate on your precepts and consider your ways.

¹⁶ I delight in your decrees; I will not neglect your word.

— Psalm 119:9-16

Remember your Creator in the days of your youth, before the days of trouble come and the years approach when you will say, "I find no pleasure in them"—

— Ecclesiastes 12:1

God's Law Is a Delight - Day Five

Read: Psalm 119:41-48 • Isaiah 54:10 • Matthew 10:18-20

In this stanza of Psalm 119, the psalmist celebrates the unfailing love of the Lord. God's promises, revealed in His Law, can be depended upon.

• **What** does the psalmist ask the Lord in Psalm 119:41, and what is his petition based upon?

• **In** Isaiah 54:10, how does God confirm this confidence?

• **In** Psalm 119:42-44, what does the psalmist's trust in God's Word allow him to do?

• **Has** anyone ever criticized you for trying to live according to God's Word? How did you answer them?

- **From** Psalm 119:45, what does the psalmist experience because he tries to live by God's precepts?

In Psalm 119:46-48, the psalmist says he is able to speak of God's revelation "before kings" without being "put to shame."

- **In** your life today, what types of people would be difficult for you to witness to? Have you spoken to them about God? What happened?

- **In** Matthew 10:18-20, Jesus warns His disciples about being brought before governors and kings as witnesses to the truth about Him. What were they not to worry about, and why?

- **How** have you experienced this provision from God as you speak about Jesus to other people?

Today's Bible Reading

[41] *May your unfailing love come to me, Lord, your salvation, according to your promise;*
[42] *then I can answer anyone who taunts me, for I trust in your word.*
[43] *Never take your word of truth from my mouth, for I have put my hope in your laws.*
[44] *I will always obey your law, for ever and ever.*
[45] *I will walk about in freedom, for I have sought out your precepts.*
[46] *I will speak of your statutes before kings and will not be put to shame,*
[47] *for I delight in your commands because I love them.*
[48] *I reach out for your commands, which I love, that I may meditate on your decrees.*

— Psalm 119:41-48

Though the mountains be shaken and the hills be removed, yet my unfailing love for you will not be shaken nor my covenant of peace be removed," says the Lord, who has compassion on you.

— Isaiah 54:10

[18] *On my account you will be brought before governors and kings as witnesses to them and to the Gentiles.*
[19] *But when they arrest you, do not worry about what to say or how to say it. At that time you will be given what to say,* [20] *for it will not be you speaking, but the Spirit of your Father speaking through you.*

— Matthew 10:18-20

God's Law Is a Delight - Day Six

Read: Psalm 119:129-136

In this stanza, the psalmist describes God's statutes and how he longs both to obey them himself and to lead others to follow them.

- **How** does the psalmist describe God's Word in verse 129, and what does this knowledge cause him to do?

- **What** does God's Word do for even the "simple"—those who are not experienced in the realities of life? (verse 130)

- **In** verse 131, how does the psalmist describe his longing for God's commands? What picture does this suggest to you?

- **List** the ways the psalmist asks for God's blessing in verses 132-135.

The psalmist trusts God to do these things "as you *always* do to those who love your name" (verse 132, italics added).

- **Do** you love God's name and have this kind of trust in Him? Write a list of ways that you would like to ask for His blessing in your own life.

- **Why** does the psalmist express deep sorrow in verse 136?

- **How** do you feel about the rebellion against God by the lost people that you see around you today? Write down a prayer to Him about them here.

Today's Bible Reading

[129] Your statutes are wonderful; therefore I obey them.

[130] The unfolding of your words gives light; it gives understanding to the simple.

[131] I open my mouth and pant, longing for your commands.

[132] Turn to me and have mercy on me, as you always do to those who love your name.

[133] Direct my footsteps according to your word; let no sin rule over me.

[134] Redeem me from human oppression, that I may obey your precepts.

[135] Make your face shine on your servant and teach me your decrees.

[136] Streams of tears flow from my eyes, for your law is not obeyed.

— Psalm 119:129-136

God's Law Is a Delight - Day Seven

Take a few minutes today to review the Bible verses from this week. Write down what has been most meaningful to you.

We hope you are learning to delight in God's Word, and in all its benefits to you.

Lesson 5 — God Supports His King

- · The King suffered for us.
- · The King is our Messiah.
- · The King is our High Priest.
- · The King is the Son of Man.
- · The King is the Son of God.
- · The King will return in judgment and redemption.

৵৹৵৻

Remember, as you work through each day's study, pray and ask God to help you know, understand, and apply His truth to your life.

God Supports His King - Day One

Read: Psalm 22:1a, 6-8, 14-18

Jesus often quoted from the Psalms and taught His disciples to interpret the Scriptures in light of His coming (see Luke 24:46-47). All the psalms, but especially the messianic psalms, relate to Jesus as King.

Psalm 22, originally written of King David, also foretells the suffering that God's coming eternal King would endure. The verses we will consider are printed on the next page.

• **Jesus,** who was fully Man as well as fully God, suffered for us in His humanity. In Matthew 27:46, He cried out as He hung upon the cross, quoting Psalm 22:1a. What was this anguished cry?

• **What** does the psalmist experience from other people in Psalm 22:6-8?

• **If** you would like to, read Matthew 27:39-43 to see how Jesus experienced similar scorn and mocking when He was crucified.

• **In** Psalm 22:14-18, how did the psalmist describe his continued righteous suffering at the hands of his enemies?

These verses also foretold Jesus' suffering for us. If you would like to, read the following passages to see how each foretold Jesus' death.

• **Psalm** 22:15 with John 19:28-30

• **Psalm** 22:16b with John 20:24-28

• **Psalm** 22:18 with Matthew 27:35

In Psalm 22:22-31, King David praised the Lord for listening to his cry for help. God also supported His Son Jesus, the King, by raising Him from death (see Matthew 28:1-10).

• **Do** you trust that God will answer your cry for help? Why not pray about this now?

Today's Bible Reading

My God, my God, why have you forsaken me?

— Psalm 22:1a

⁶ But I am a worm and not a man, scorned by everyone, despised by the people.

⁷ All who see me mock me; they hurl insults, shaking their heads.

⁸ "He trusts in the Lord," they say, "let the Lord rescue him. Let him deliver him, since he delights in him."

— Psalm 22:6-8

¹⁴ I am poured out like water, and all my bones are out of joint. My heart has turned to wax; it has melted within me.

¹⁵ My mouth is dried up like a potsherd, and my tongue sticks to the roof of my mouth; you lay me in the dust of death.

¹⁶ Dogs surround me, a pack of villains encircles me; they pierce my hands and my feet.

¹⁷ All my bones are on display; people stare and gloat over me.

¹⁸ They divide my clothes among them and cast lots for my garment.

— Psalm 22:14-18

Additional reading:
Psalm 22:22-31
Matthew 27:35,39-43,46
Matthew 28:1-10
Luke 24:46-47
John 19:28-30
John 20:24-28

God Supports His King - Day Two

Read: Psalm 110

Jesus and His apostles quoted from Psalm 110 to show how the Messiah had been foretold in Scripture.

- **What** promise did God make to King David and his dynasty, which would culminate in the Messiah, in Psalm 110:1? (Jesus quoted this verse in Matthew 22:41-46, and Peter quoted it in Acts 2:32-36.)

- **How** would the Lord give strength and authority to His king, first to David, and later to the Messiah-King, according to Psalm 110:2-3?

- **What** unchanging oath did the Lord swear to King David in Psalm 110:4?[1] (The writer of Hebrews discussed this oath and applied it to Jesus as our great high priest in Hebrews 4:14—5:10 and 6:16—7:28.)

---

[1] Melchizedek was the king-priest of God Most High at Jerusalem in the days of Abraham (see Genesis 14:18,20). As such a king-priest, he was appointed to a higher order of priesthood than that of Aaron and his sons. [*The NIV Study Bible* (Grand Rapids: Zondervan, 2011)]

- **From** Psalm 110:5-7, how will the Lord bring victory to His King?

If you have time, read Revelation 19:11-21, which describes the Lord's final judgment of the nations, carried out by Jesus Christ, the Messiah and King.

This final battle will be a terrifying event in the future, but if you belong to Jesus, you have nothing to fear. (If you aren't sure, see page 4 to find out how you can become His.)

- **God** put so much of Himself into every word of Scripture, so that His people could come to know Him. How does it make you feel to see His plan for a Messiah-King unfolding in the Psalms, and then see its fulfillment in the New Testament?

Today's Bible Reading

[1] *The Lord says to my lord: "Sit at my right hand until I make your enemies a footstool for your feet."*

[2] *The Lord will extend your mighty scepter from Zion, saying, "Rule in the midst of your enemies!"*

[3] *Your troops will be willing on your day of battle. Arrayed in holy splendor, your young men will come to you like dew from the morning's womb.*

[4] *The Lord has sworn and will not change his mind: "You are a priest forever, in the order of Melchizedek."*

[5] *The Lord is at your right hand; he will crush kings on the day of his wrath.*

[6] *He will judge the nations, heaping up the dead and crushing the rulers of the whole earth.*

[7] *He will drink from a brook along the way, and so he will lift his head high.*

— Psalm 110

Additional reading:
Matthew 22:41-46
Acts 2:32-36
Hebrews 4:14—5:10
Hebrews 6:16—7:28
Revelation 19:11-21

God Supports His King - Day Three

Read: Psalm 95:7b-11 • Hebrews 3:1 • Hebrews 4:9-11,14,16

The apostles used the Psalms to establish Jesus' priestly ministry to believers.

• **What** did the psalmist beg God's people to do in Psalm 95:7b?

• **What** example from Israel's history did he cite in Psalm 95:8-11?

God had done mighty works to take Israel out of slavery in Egypt and had taken them safely through the wilderness, yet they complained and rebelled against Him.

• **The** writer of Hebrews quoted Psalm 95:7b-11 in Hebrews 3:7-11. In Hebrews 3:1, how does he open his discussion of this psalm?

- **In** Hebrews chapters 3-4, the writer demonstrates that Moses, Joshua, and King David were not able to provide true "rest" for God's people. What does Hebrews 4:9-11 urge us to do in order to enter God's true rest?[1]

- **From** Hebrews 4:14,16, by whose provision are we able to do this?

Jesus, our King and High Priest, gave Himself as the final sacrifice for our sin. All we need to do is believe in Him and accept His gift, in order to enter God's rest.

- **Have** you accepted His gift by faith and rested from your works? Write down what this means to you.

---

[1] God's rest is a new relationship with God that means the cessation of works and legalism as a way to please God. We have peace with God by faith in Jesus Christ (see Romans 5:1), we are free from guilt, and our sin is forgiven. And it means we can totally depend on God for everything we need.

Today's Bible Reading

[7] ...Today, if only you would hear his voice,

[8] "Do not harden your hearts as you did at Meribah, as you did that day at Massah in the wilderness, [9] where your ancestors tested me; they tried me, though they had seen what I did.

[10] For forty years I was angry with that generation; I said, 'They are a people whose hearts go astray, and they have not known my ways.'

[11] So I declared on oath in my anger, 'They shall never enter my rest.'"
— Psalm 95:7b-11

Therefore...fix your thoughts on Jesus, whom we acknowledge as our apostle and high priest.
— Hebrews 3:1

[9] There remains, then, a Sabbath-rest for the people of God; [10] for anyone who enters God's rest also rests from their works, just as God did from his. [11] Let us, therefore, make every effort to enter that rest, so that no one will perish by following their example of disobedience.
— Hebrews 4:9-11

[14] Therefore, since we have a great high priest who has ascended into heaven, Jesus the Son of God, let us hold firmly to the faith we profess...[16] Let us then approach God's throne of grace with confidence, so that we may receive mercy and find grace to help us in our time of need.
— Hebrews 4:14,16

God Supports His King - Day Four

Read: Psalm 16:5-11

The apostles quoted from Psalm 16 to show that Jesus is the Son of Man, according to the Scriptures.

- **First,** we will look at what the original author said. How does King David, the psalmist, express his confidence in the Lord in Psalm 16:5-8?

- **From** Psalm 16:9-10, having experienced God's care for him throughout his life, where else is David confident that God will protect him?

- **What** is the present experience and the ultimate goal of David's life? (Psalm 16:11)

In the Book of Acts, both the Apostle Peter and the Apostle Paul said that since King David himself did not rise from the grave, Psalm 16 looked forward to Jesus, the Son of David, rising from the dead.

- **Peter** quoted Psalm 16:8-11 in Acts 2:25-28. He then explained why these words written by David applied to Jesus Christ. If you have time, read and summarize what he said in Acts 2:29-32.

- **Paul** quoted Psalm 16:10 in Acts 13:35. If you have time, read Acts 13:32-39. How did Paul establish that the Scriptures foretold the resurrection of Jesus?

Because of Jesus' resurrection, Christians can be confident that He will not abandon them in death. Not only our souls, but even our bodies will be resurrected to eternal life.

- **Do** you have this confidence? If you're not sure, see page 4. Write down your thoughts about this.

Today's Bible Reading

⁵ *Lord, you alone are my portion and my cup; you make my lot secure.*

⁶ *The boundary lines have fallen for me in pleasant places; surely I have a delightful inheritance.*

⁷ *I will praise the Lord, who counsels me; even at night my heart instructs me.*

⁸ *I keep my eyes always on the Lord. With him at my right hand, I will not be shaken.*

⁹ *Therefore my heart is glad and my tongue rejoices; my body also will rest secure,*

¹⁰ *because you will not abandon me to the realm of the dead, nor will you let your faithful one see decay.*

¹¹ *You make known to me the path of life; you will fill me with joy in your presence, with eternal pleasures at your right hand.*

— Psalm 16:5-11

Additional reading:
Acts 2:25-32
Acts 13:32-39

God Supports His King - Day Five

Read: Psalm 2

Psalm 2 is one of the psalms most quoted in the New Testament. In it we find scriptural confirmation of the King's identity as God's Son.

- **From** Psalm 2:1-3, what is the attitude of the rulers of the earth towards God and His King?

- **From** verses 4-5, is the Lord worried about this rebellion? What is His response in verse 6?

- **What** was God's decree, first to King David but ultimately to the coming Messiah-King, in verses 7-9?

- **If** you have time, read Matthew 3:16-17. What did God the Father proclaim at Jesus' baptism?

- **If** you have time, read Hebrews 1:1-5. The writer confirms Jesus' identity as God's Son, quoting Psalm 2:7 in verse 5. Where does Hebrews 1:3 say the Son of God is now seated?

- **How** does Psalm 2:10-12 look forward to the rule of God's Son on earth?

Jesus taught us to pray, "Your kingdom come" (Matthew 6:10). This is the kingdom of God's Son that we look forward to. (See Revelation 21:3-4.)

- **When** you pray, do you pray for those who continue their rebellion against God? What else can you do to help those who don't know Jesus as their Savior to come to Him in faith?

Today's Bible Reading

¹ Why do the nations conspire and the peoples plot in vain?

² The kings of the earth rise up and the rulers band together against the Lord and against his anointed, saying,

³ "Let us break their chains and throw off their shackles."

⁴ The One enthroned in heaven laughs; the Lord scoffs at them.

⁵ He rebukes them in his anger and terrifies them in his wrath, saying,

⁶ "I have installed my king on Zion, my holy mountain. "

⁷ I will proclaim the Lord's decree: He said to me, "You are my son; today I have become your father.

⁸ Ask me, and I will make the nations your inheritance, the ends of the earth your possession.

⁹ You will break them with a rod of iron; you will dash them to pieces like pottery. "

¹⁰ Therefore, you kings, be wise; be warned, you rulers of the earth.

¹¹ Serve the Lord with fear and celebrate his rule with trembling.

¹² Kiss his son, or he will be angry and your way will lead to your destruction, for his wrath can flare up in a moment. Blessed are all who take refuge in him.

— Psalm 2

Additional reading:
Matthew 3:16-17
Matthew 6:9-13
Hebrews 1:1-5
Revelation 21:3-4

God Supports His King - Day Six

Read: Psalm 96

Many psalms looked forward to the King's return to deliver His people while judging the nations. Today we will look at Psalm 96 in that light.

- **From** Psalm 96:1-3, what are God's people called to sing?

The consummation of this call is reflected in Revelation 5:9 and 14:3, in which all who stand before God's throne sing a "new song" of praise to Jesus Christ, the Lamb of God who gave His life for our salvation.

- **How** does the psalmist describe the greatness of God in Psalm 96:4-6?

- **In** Psalm 96:7-9, who else is invited to acknowledge God's greatness?

- **Who** rules the world, and is therefore qualified to judge the peoples of the earth? (Psalm 96:10)

• **How** does Psalm 96:11-13a call all of creation to react to the coming of the King to judge the earth?

• **From** Psalm 96:13b, on what basis will the King pass judgment?

In Acts 17:31, the Apostle Paul said, "For he has set a day when he will judge the world with justice by the man he has appointed. He has given proof of this to everyone by raising him from the dead."

• **Will** you rejoice with God's people and all of creation when the Lord Jesus returns to deliver His people and to judge the nations? Write down your thoughts here.

Today's Bible Reading

¹ Sing to the Lord a new song; sing to the Lord, all the earth.

² Sing to the Lord, praise his name; proclaim his salvation day after day.

³ Declare his glory among the nations, his marvelous deeds among all peoples.

⁴ For great is the Lord and most worthy of praise; he is to be feared above all gods.

⁵ For all the gods of the nations are idols, but the Lord made the heavens.

⁶ Splendor and majesty are before him; strength and glory are in his sanctuary.

⁷ Ascribe to the Lord, all you families of nations, ascribe to the Lord glory and strength.

⁸ Ascribe to the Lord the glory due his name; bring an offering and come into his courts.

⁹ Worship the Lord in the splendor of his holiness; tremble before him, all the earth.

¹⁰ Say among the nations, "The Lord reigns." The world is firmly established, it cannot be moved; he will judge the peoples with equity.

¹¹ Let the heavens rejoice, let the earth be glad; let the sea resound, and all that is in it.

¹² Let the fields be jubilant, and everything in them; let all the trees of the forest sing for joy.

¹³ Let all creation rejoice before the Lord, for he comes, he comes to judge the earth. He will judge the world in righteousness and the peoples in his faithfulness.

— Psalm 96

God Supports His King - Day Seven

Take a few minutes today to review the Bible verses from this week. Write down what has been most meaningful to you.

We hope you have accepted Jesus Christ as your Savior, the sacrifice for your sin, and are looking forward to His return. (See page 4 for additional information about this.)

Lesson 6 — God Watches Over the Redeemed

- He is the Redeemer of His people.
- He leads them to a place to settle.
- He sends His Word to heal them.
- He controls life's storms.
- He works all things for their good.
- He is their Shepherd.

తిల్ప

Remember, as you work through each day's study, pray and ask God to help you know, understand, and apply His truth to your life.

God Watches Over the Redeemed - Day One

Read: Psalm 105:1-11

Today we will see that God is the Redeemer of His people—first the people of Israel, and also His people from all nations.

- **What** does the psalmist call for and in what ways? (Psalm 105:1-5)

- **To** whom is the psalmist speaking? (Psalm 105:6)

- **From** Psalm 105:7-11, with whom did God make a covenant, and how long will that covenant stand?

- **If** you have time, read Genesis 17:7; 22:15-18; 26:2-4; and Leviticus 26:42-45. Who made the promise, oath, or covenant, and therefore upon whom does its fulfillment depend?

In the New Testament, we find that God remembered His covenant and sent His Son, Jesus Christ. Through Jesus, we are heirs of the new covenant the Lord made with people from all nations who will seek His face.

- **If** you would like to, read Luke 1:68-79. How does Zechariah, the father of John the Baptist, confirm the way God was fulfilling His promise?

- **Zechariah** said that Jesus Christ came "to shine on those living in darkness and in the shadow of death, to guide our feet into the path of peace" (Luke 1:79). Have you entered "the path of peace" by accepting Jesus as your Savior? (See page 4 for more information.) Whom do you know that lives "in darkness and in the shadow of death" that needs to hear about Jesus? What will you do about it?

Today's Bible Reading

[1] Give praise to the Lord, proclaim his name; make known among the nations what he has done.

[2] Sing to him, sing praise to him; tell of all his wonderful acts.

[3] Glory in his holy name; let the hearts of those who seek the Lord rejoice.

[4] Look to the Lord and his strength; seek his face always.

[5] Remember the wonders he has done, his miracles, and the judgments he pronounced,

[6] you his servants, the descendants of Abraham, his chosen ones, the children of Jacob.

[7] He is the Lord our God; his judgments are in all the earth.

[8] He remembers his covenant forever, the promise he made, for a thousand generations,

[9] the covenant he made with Abraham, the oath he swore to Isaac.

[10] He confirmed it to Jacob as a decree, to Israel as an everlasting covenant:

[11] "To you I will give the land of Canaan as the portion you will inherit."

— Psalm 105:1-11

Additional reading:
Genesis 17:7
Genesis 22:15-18
Genesis 26:2-4
Leviticus 26:42-45
Luke 1:68-79

God Watches Over the Redeemed - Day Two

Read: Psalm 107:1-9

Psalm 107 lists cases where the Lord delivered His redeemed from all kinds of need. We will look at one example of His deliverance today.

• **In** Psalm 107:1, why does the psalmist call us to give thanks to the Lord?

• **Whom** does he call upon to tell their stories in verses 2-3?

• **What** example does the psalmist give of the afflictions suffered by God's people in verses 4-5?

This could refer to Israel's wilderness wanderings after they left Egypt. However, it could also describe any person who lives aimlessly with no purpose or destination.

• **From** verse 6a, what did the wanderers do?

- **How** did the Lord respond? (verses 6b-7)

- **What** are they called to do, and why? (verses 8-9)

God in His unfailing love always answers His people when they pray to Him in their trouble. He does wonderful things in answer to prayer.

- **Have** you experienced being lost, hungry and thirsty, whether spiritually, emotionally, or materially? Did you cry out to the Lord? How did He respond?

- **Whom** do you know who may be experiencing these kinds of afflictions today? How will you encourage them to turn to the Lord?

Today's Bible Reading

[1] Give thanks to the Lord, for he is good; his love endures forever.

[2] Let the redeemed of the Lord tell their story—those he redeemed from the hand of the foe,

[3] those he gathered from the lands, from east and west, from north and south.

[4] Some wandered in desert wastelands, finding no way to a city where they could settle.

[5] They were hungry and thirsty, and their lives ebbed away.

[6] Then they cried out to the Lord in their trouble, and he delivered them from their distress.

[7] He led them by a straight way to a city where they could settle.

[8] Let them give thanks to the Lord for his unfailing love and his wonderful deeds for mankind,

[9] for he satisfies the thirsty and fills the hungry with good things.

— Psalm 107:1-9

God Watches Over the Redeemed - Day Three

Read: Psalm 107:17-22 • Galatians 6:7-8 • John 1:1,12

Since we already studied Psalm 107:10-16 in Lesson 1, we will move on to verses 17-22 today.

• **In** Psalm 107:17-18, what happened to some of the redeemed, and why?

• **How** did the Apostle Paul express the inevitable consequences of those who rebel against God's way in Galatians 6:7-8?

• **Even** though a person rebels, that doesn't have to seal their fate forever. What did the rebellious ones do in Psalm 107:19a?

• **How** did God respond? (Psalm 107:19b-20)

A person who rebels against the Word of the Lord—His law—is condemned by that law. But when they cry to the Lord, His Word becomes their healing and salvation.

- **What** do you learn about this Word in John 1:1,12?

The Apostle John goes on to say in John 1:17, "For the law was given through Moses; grace and truth came through Jesus Christ."

- **In** Psalm 107:21-22, what are the redeemed urged to do?

- **Have** you cried to the Lord and been redeemed by the blood of Jesus? What thank offerings might you offer to Him? Whom will you tell of His works?

Today's Bible Reading

17 Some became fools through their rebellious ways and suffered affliction because of their iniquities.

18 They loathed all food and drew near the gates of death.

19 Then they cried to the Lord in their trouble, and he saved them from their distress.

20 He sent out his word and healed them; he rescued them from the grave.

21 Let them give thanks to the Lord for his unfailing love and his wonderful deeds for mankind.

22 Let them sacrifice thank offerings and tell of his works with songs of joy.

— Psalm 107:17-22

7 Do not be deceived: God cannot be mocked. A man reaps what he sows.
8 Whoever sows to please their flesh, from the flesh will reap destruction; whoever sows to please the Spirit, from the Spirit will reap eternal life.

— Galatians 6:7-8

1 In the beginning was the Word, and the Word was with God, and the Word was God...12 Yet to all who did receive him, to those who believed in his name, he gave the right to become children of God...

— John 1:1,12

Additional reading:
John 1:17

God Watches Over the Redeemed - Day Four

Read: Psalm 107:23-32

In today's passage, we will see yet another way that God cares for the redeemed.

- **Whom** does the psalmist introduce, and what do they see in Psalm 107:23-24?

- **How** did the storm arise? (verse 25)

- **How** were they affected, and what did they do then? (verses 26-28a)

- **What** did the Lord do in response? (verses 28b-30)

- **What** does the psalmist call on them to do? (verses 31-32)

God's power allows Him to both stir up a storm and then calm it. He is in control of nature.

- **If** you have time, read Jonah chapter 1 and Matthew 8:23-27. How is the Lord's power over the storm revealed in these passages?

God not only controls nature; He also controls every aspect of life because He is sovereign (see Lesson 1).

- **What** does this knowledge mean to you? Are you facing storms of life that make you feel at your wits' end? What will you do now?

Today's Bible Reading

²³ Some went out on the sea in ships; they were merchants on the mighty waters.

²⁴ They saw the works of the Lord, his wonderful deeds in the deep.

²⁵ For he spoke and stirred up a tempest that lifted high the waves.

²⁶ They mounted up to the heavens and went down to the depths; in their peril their courage melted away.

²⁷ They reeled and staggered like drunkards; they were at their wits' end.

²⁸ Then they cried out to the Lord in their trouble, and he brought them out of their distress.

²⁹ He stilled the storm to a whisper; the waves of the sea were hushed.

³⁰ They were glad when it grew calm, and he guided them to their desired haven.

³¹ Let them give thanks to the Lord for his unfailing love and his wonderful deeds for mankind.

³² Let them exalt him in the assembly of the people and praise him in the council of the elders.

— Psalm 107:23-32

Additional reading:
Jonah 1
Matthew 8:23-27

God Watches Over the Redeemed - Day Five

Read: Psalm 107:33-43 • Romans 8:28

The psalmist ends Psalm 107 with additional reasons that the redeemed can thank and praise the Lord.

• **In** Psalm 107:33-34 and 39-40, what does the Lord do in response to the wicked who prosper in their God-given land?

• **How** does the Lord transform the desert to benefit those who trust in Him? (Psalm 107:35-38,41)

• **How** do those who witness these things respond? (Psalm 107:42)

• **Why** should a person study the acts of the Lord in human history? (Psalm 107:43)

Psalm 107 shows us that God blesses the redeemed—they can trust in Him even when they are going through adversity. But God's judgment will certainly fall on those who exalt themselves and do not acknowledge His blessings.

- **By** doing this Bible study, you are studying what God has been doing throughout human history. This is the path to godly wisdom. How do you think it is helping you to know God better?

- **Read** Romans 8:28. Have you learned to trust that God will work all things for your good? How have you seen this in your life in the past? In what present situation do you need to trust Him?

Today's Bible Reading

33 He turned rivers into a desert, flowing springs into thirsty ground,

34 and fruitful land into a salt waste, because of the wickedness of those who lived there.

35 He turned the desert into pools of water and the parched ground into flowing springs;

36 there he brought the hungry to live, and they founded a city where they could settle.

37 They sowed fields and planted vineyards that yielded a fruitful harvest;

38 he blessed them, and their numbers greatly increased, and he did not let their herds diminish.

39 Then their numbers decreased, and they were humbled by oppression, calamity and sorrow;

40 he who pours contempt on nobles made them wander in a trackless waste.

41 But he lifted the needy out of their affliction and increased their families like flocks.

42 The upright see and rejoice, but all the wicked shut their mouths.

43 Let the one who is wise heed these things and ponder the loving deeds of the Lord.

— Psalm 107:33-43

And we know that in all things God works for the good of those who love him, who have been called according to his purpose.

— Romans 8:28

God Watches Over the Redeemed - Day Six

Read: Psalm 23 • John 10:11,14 • Revelation 7:17

Psalm 23 is one of the most beloved psalms.

• **How** does the psalmist characterize the Lord in Psalm 23:1a?

• **In** what way does God provide for the needs of His people? (Psalm 23:1b-3a)

• **How** does the Lord guide, protect, and comfort His people? (Psalm 23:3b-4)

• **In** what way does God give the best to His people? (Psalm 23:5)

• **What** conclusion does the psalmist reach in Psalm 23:6?

- **Jesus,** God's Son, also taught that we can have this kind of relationship with Him. What did He say in John 10:11,14?

- **The** Apostle John looked forward to the glory God was preparing for His people. What did he tell us in Revelation 7:17? If you have time, read all of Revelation 7:10-17 to see the full picture.

- **Do** you know that the Lord is your Shepherd? How has He provided for your needs, guided, protected, and comforted you? Share with your group if you would like to.

Today's Bible Reading

[1] The Lord is my shepherd, I lack nothing.

[2] He makes me lie down in green pastures, he leads me beside quiet waters,

[3] he refreshes my soul. He guides me along the right paths for his name's sake.

[4] Even though I walk through the darkest valley, I will fear no evil, for you are with me; your rod and your staff, they comfort me.

[5] You prepare a table before me in the presence of my enemies. You anoint my head with oil; my cup overflows.

[6] Surely your goodness and love will follow me all the days of my life, and I will dwell in the house of the Lord forever.

— Psalm 23

[11] I am the good shepherd. The good shepherd lays down his life for the sheep…
[14] I am the good shepherd; I know my sheep and my sheep know me.

— John 10:11,14

For the Lamb at the center of the throne will be their shepherd; "he will lead them to springs of living water."

"And God will wipe away every tear from their eyes."

— Revelation 7:17

Additional reading:
Revelation 7:10-17

God Supports the Redeemed - Day Seven

Take a few minutes today to review the Bible verses from this week. Write down what has been most meaningful to you.

Because God is infinite and His Word is living, you can spend the rest of your life growing to know Him better as you study His Word. If you have accepted Jesus Christ as your Savior—as the sacrifice for your sin—then you have become a child of God and have started on this wonderful journey of knowing God. *Joy of Living* has many studies that will help you on your journey.